BE SAFE AROUND
STRANGERS

BRIDGET HEOS   ILLUSTRATED BY SILVIA BARONCELLI

RiverStream Illustrated
Great Reading • Real Learning

Amicus Illustrated hardcover edition is published by Amicus
P.O. Box 1329, Mankato, MN 56002
www.amicuspublishing.us

RiverStream Publishing reprinted with permission of
Amicus Publishing.

Library of Congress Cataloging-in-Publication Data
Heos, Bridget.
 Be safe around strangers / by Bridget Heos; illustrated by
Silvia Baroncelli.
    pages cm. — (Be safe!)
 Includes bibliographical references.
 Summary: "Carlos walks home from school with his younger
friend Pablo and teaches him which strangers are safe to ask
for help and which aren't"— Provided by publisher.
 Audience: Grade K to 3.
 ISBN 978-1-60753-447-1 (library binding) —
ISBN 978-1-60753-662-8 (ebook)
 1. Children and strangers–Juvenile literature. 2. Safety
education—Juvenile literature. 3. Crime prevention—Juvenile
literature. I. Baroncelli, Silvia, illustrator. II. Title.
 HQ784.S8H46 2015
 613.60835—dc23   2013032440

Editor: Rebecca Glaser
Designer: Kathleen Petelinsek

1 2 3 4 5 CG 18 17 16 15 14
RiverStream Publishing–Corporate Graphics,
Mankato, MN—042014
ISBN 978-1-62243-260-8 (paperback)

ABOUT THE AUTHOR

Bridget Heos is the author of more than 60 children's books, including many advice and how-to titles. She lives safely in Kansas City with her husband and four children. You can find out more about her at www.authorbridgetheos.com.

ABOUT THE ILLUSTRATOR

Silvia Baroncelli has loved to draw since she was a child. She collaborates regularly with publishers in drawing and graphic design from her home in Prato, Italy. Her best collaborators are her four nephews, daughter Ginevra, and organized husband Tommaso. Find out more about her on the web at silviabaroncelli.it

"Stranger Danger! Stranger Danger!"
"Pablo, what are you doing?"
"I'm pointing out all the strangers, Carlos. So we know who to stay away from."

"Well, not all strangers are bad, Pablo. Most people are nice. But you do have to watch out for strangers acting strangely.

You also have to watch out for people you know who act strangely. I'll give you some tips on the way home."

"So, Pablo, let's say one of these drivers stopped and asked you for directions. Grown-ups aren't supposed to ask kids for directions, so that's strange. You should tell a grown-up."

"Who should I tell, Carlos?
All I see are strangers."

"This is a crossing guard, Pablo. He is a stranger. But he is also a community helper. People like crossing guards and police officers can help you. So you could tell him."

"Do you know him, Pablo?"
"I forgot his name. He came to our block party."
"Okay. What if he offered us a ride?"
"I'd say yes. He's not a stranger. He's the guy from the party."

"You should say no, Pablo. You only *sort of* know him. Never get in a car with someone you don't know well. Even if they say your parents said to, don't go. Your parents wouldn't send a stranger—or someone you barely know—to pick you up."

"You need a Band-Aid."

"I see someone inside that house. Maybe they have one."

"We don't know the people in that house, Pablo. Let's go to the library instead."

"Yes, she's a stranger, Pablo. But this is a public place. And she works here. It's safe to ask workers for help in a public place."

There, that's better.

"You can also go to a house where you know the person, Pablo. But remember, even people you know can act strange."

Hey, I've got some candy for you kids.

Pablo says, "I'll be right there."

But Carlos says, "No thanks! We have to get home."

"Aw. Come on," says the neighbor.

"Nope! See you later!" says Carlos.

"But we know him, Carlos. He goes to our church."
"I know. But I feel weird around that guy. I don't want to be with him without a grown-up. I talked to my mom about it. She says it's smart to trust your instincts."

"But I think we hurt his feelings."
"He'll be fine. It's okay to tell a grown-up no, Pablo. It's okay to be assertive."

"Hi, Mom," says Pablo.
"Hi, Mrs. Gomez," says Carlos.
"What happened to your knee?" Mrs. Gomez asks.

"I fell in the rain and cut it. We got a Band-Aid from a stranger. But it's okay, because we were in a public place. And she was a librarian."

"Smart thinking, kiddo," his mom says.

"Thanks, Mom. You know, not all strangers are bad."

SAFETY RULES TO REMEMBER

- Walk and play with a friend or a group instead of alone.
- Most strangers are nice people. But be wary of strangers—or people you know—who are acting strange, or make you feel uncomfortable. Tell a parent, community helper, or trusted adult if this happens.
- Never get in a car with a stranger or someone you don't know well.
- Always tell your parents where you are.
- If you need help, go to a public place, or ask a community helper like a crossing guard or police officer.
- It's okay to be assertive to grown-ups. You can tell them no, and if you are in danger, yell and scream for help.

GLOSSARY WORDS

assertive Being confident and brave when you say something.

community helper A worker, such as a police officer, crossing guard, or nurse, who helps others in the community.

instinct A feeling you have about something, such as the feeling that something is unsafe.

public place A building or outside area where anyone can gather.

trusted adult An adult whom you know and who would help you and take care of you if needed.

READ MORE

Donahue, Jill Urban. Say No and Go: Stranger Safety. How to Be Safe! Minneapolis: Picture Window Books, 2009.

Guard, Anara. What if a Stranger Approaches You? Mankato, Minn.: Picture Window Books, 2012.

Herrington, Lisa M. Stranger Safety. New York: Children's Press, 2013.

WEBSITES

FBI–KIDS SAFETY
http://www.fbi.gov/fun-games/kids/kids-sa
Learn safety tips from the FBI.

SAFETY: GIRLS HEALTH
http://www.girlshealth.gov/safety/index.ht
This website offers safety tips for girls.

STREET SMART KIDZ SAFETY PROGRAM
http://www.streetsmartkidz.ca/
Learn more about standing up for yoursel
and keeping yourself safe.

Every effort has been made to ensure that these websites are appropriate for children. However, because of the nature of the Internet, it is impossible to guarantee that these sites will remain acti indefinitely or that their contents will not be altered.